FROM
PRISON *to*
PROMISE

SONYA STAPLES

Publisher: VOG Publishing

Dedication

Over the years, life has thrown me many curve balls. But through it all, I learned the lessons they aimed to teach. I want to dedicate this book to everyone who holds a special place in my heart.

To God, I THANK YOU! To my parents Donna Clay and Ervin Hart Jr and my late grandparents Merrix and Willie Mae Wilson, thank you for shaping my foundation and loving me through the good and the bad. Things haven't been perfect with us, but we have grown through the tough times and for that I am grateful. To my children for always having my back and making me feel like the best mother in the world.

Finally, my wonderful loving husband. Jonathan, YOU ARE MY WORLD. Thank you for loving me through my darkest times. You inspire me to keep pushing. I LOVE YOU ALL.

"I feel like since I can't have you in my life, then life isn't worth living anymore."

Hearing those words after so many years of separating myself from him cut me deep. I never considered his feelings. I knew I was at my breaking point. Life alone was not easy and living life without him proved to be much harder.

When this journey started, I determined to be all in! I was going to be a ride or die chick who stood by her man. Things started crumbling fast, and I had no idea what to do. We were only teens when our story began, he was 17, and I was 16. Two young souls were doing adult things, two diverse backgrounds, two different paths, the SAME PAIN. I had no idea when we met our lives would take the turn it did. But looking back, everything we lived through was necessary.

Chapter one

It's only right for me to start from the beginning, my story. I was born in 1979 to a young mother and a drug-dealing and drug-using father. My grandparents on my mother's side knew my parents were not ready for a child. They had issues of their own, trying to live life. So, my grandparents stepped in to raise me. I lived in a house in a good neighborhood, with a woman and a man raising me. My grandfather worked and provided for the entire household, and my grandmother kept house and made sure things stayed in order. Not to mention the fact that I rarely had to ask for anything. If I did what they expected of me, they rewarded me double. I couldn't ask for anything better.

My grandparents were awesome. They showed up at all my recitals, organized great birthday parties, and exposed me to things my schoolmates were not doing. I can remember fishing trips with them, me being too scared to bait the hook and my grandfather would step in. I was also afraid to take the fish off the hook, but they made such a big deal of me holding the line and reeling in my catch, I thought I was the best! That's what life was like for me. Making a big deal over the little things and yet providing a strong foundation to shape me into a responsible adult. I would spend time with my mom, as well. My dad stayed in and out of prison and rehab. But I was so used to the comfort and safety at my grandparents' house, so I chose to stay there.

My grandparents were the glue to the family. They made sure we held firm to our family ties despite who messed up. They also adopted a lot of people into the family, which made holidays and cookouts that much more enjoyable. Those were perfect times. As I started to get older, so did my grandparents, of course. My mother started a relationship with a man who would soon become my sister's father. I did not like this guy at all. I was supposed to be the center of attention on our weekends. But with him being there, that wasn't the case. In my eyes, he was a jerk, and I just dealt with him through the weekend; then it was back to life.

One day, he and my mom came to my grandmother's house with the news. My mom told me she was pregnant. I didn't like it at all. How dare she have another child? Back then, I didn't see myself being spoiled or downright selfish. I just knew another baby was going to be weird.

I never really spoke about my feelings about a lot of things because I didn't believe I had the strength to do so. One day I had a friend over, and we were outside playing. She started to sing a song, and the words touched me so much I broke into tears. My grandmother asked, "Sonya, what's wrong?" "I want my mama!" I screamed. My grandmother had never raised her voice at me until I said those words. "After everything we have done for you! How dare you say that to me?" Her words crushed my heart. I didn't want to discount anything they had done. I lived a great life, but I still wanted and needed my parents. What child doesn't?

I started to pack my feelings inside. I didn't like to hurt anyone's feelings, and I couldn't articulate words accurately enough to express my point. That's where the sadness began.

My sister was born in 1988. The feelings were bizarre because as much as I despised her coming, I was excited. She promoted me to a big sister! This sense of protection overcame me when I first laid eyes on her, and the resentment fell in the shadows. When my mom brought her home, I still lived with my grandparents, and I visited on the weekends. Thinking back, that may have been enough time for me. I loved my sister, but I also loved being the "only "kid.

After about two and a half years, my haven disappeared. My father came home from prison with addiction in tow. My mom stopped dealing with my sisters' father. Before I knew it, she was back with my dad, and we were on our way to family life. I moved with my mom, dad, and sister. Life began to change. I was going through puberty, and I had difficulty adjusting to life with my parents. Life, in my eyes, started to fall apart. I attempted suicide, and I ran away. I lied, stole, and smoked weed, a complete turnaround from life at the Grands. It came to the point that there were so many problems, I couldn't identify them. I knew I didn't love myself, and I was comfortable with existing in a dark place. It seemed like it would never end. But God had a plan.

It was 1995 when I met him. I sat on the bleachers in an almost empty gymnasium, barely watching a rec basketball game. To this day, I have no idea why I was there. I wasn't interested in the game at all. I had my little sister with me, so my attention was focused more on her than watching the game. I did notice that I had eyes on me from across the court. It sounds like some mushy fairy-tale crap, but it's the truth.

When I made eye contact, my face didn't do a good job hiding the thought going through my mind, "Why the hell is he staring at me like that?" Before the idea stopped, he started walking over. "Excuse me, how are you doing? Can I talk to you?"

"I'm good, what's up?" I said with my face still screwed.

He extended his hand. "My name is Jay Jay, what's yours?

Before I answered, my sister yells, "I know him, sister! He is always at the club handing out money!" That statement put a thought in my head!

His palms were sweaty. He was nervous, so that made him kind of cute. I gave him my name, and we talked for a few. I had a screw face the entire conversation, so you can imagine how intimidating that was to this dude. Guys like him didn't usually approach me. He was very light-skinned; not my type at all! I went with the flow for the moment until I decided to leave. I thought he would take that as a hint until he followed me to my car.

"So, can I give you my beeper number?" (Yes, I said beeper!)

I smirked and answered, "Yeah, you can,"

"But will you use it?"

"Yeah, I got you!" He gave me his number, and I pulled off. I honestly thought I wouldn't see him again.

One day, maybe two weeks later, I was running very late to pick my sister up from the club. I'm flying through the west end, taking short cuts to make it on time. As I'm going down the street, who do I see as I'm approaching the next corner, Jay Jay! I tried to avoid him because I took the number, didn't call, and honestly didn't care. I flew past him and glanced in the rear mirror, and he is jumping and waving in the middle of the street to get my attention! And that was the beginning of our forever.

hapter two

I eventually transferred to the high school in the area Jay Jay lived. Once the word was out, he was my man, certain things had me wondering who I was dating. I grew up in a different part of town and a different manner than he was. I was sneaky with my endeavors even though I didn't have to do the dirt I did.

But Jay Jay was different, hell, he was already a father when we met. His family had custody, and they helped him raise his son. He lived a very adult life at an early age.

Our connection was so crazy. It was like something out of a movie. We both had an idea of the things we were into, but we never really discussed it. Jay Jay was getting money, and so was I, but when we were together, none of that even mattered. It was tough for him to figure me out. I loved how he treated me, but I still had my wall up about certain things. I would stop by to visit before going to work or after leaving school. He would sneak money in my ashtray or glove box, and it would still be there the next time I came. "Why is this still here?"

He would answer, "Why did you put it there? I don't recall asking for it." His face was priceless. Poor thing was so confused. He wasn't used to someone like me who didn't want him for his money or his street fame. But trust me that did not stop him at all. He was determined to be the last boyfriend I would ever have.

When I transferred, I knew people, but I didn't have too many meaningful relationships at the time. I was at the end of my sophomore year, so most of my friends were at my last school. I became close with a few people who helped make the transition better. Some started to not interact with me as much once they knew Jay Jay and I dated, which was fine with me. One day, I met a girl who I sparked a conversation within the cafeteria. "Are you from the West End?" she asked.

"Naw, but my boyfriend is."

"Oh, okay, what's his name?" "Jonathan, but they call him Jay Jay." Her eyes got big as quarters.

Immediately, I thought she was going to say either her or one of her girls was his girlfriend too. She said, "Ratboy? Do they call him Ratboy?"

"Ummmm, no, Jay Jay." I was green as hell!

She asked, "Light-skinned, long curly hair?"

"Yeah, why?"

"That's Ratboy! He's my cousin!"

So, all the time we spend around each other, I had never heard anyone refer to him as Ratboy. Or, maybe I never paid close attention. Besides, he never allowed me on the block, and if I did show up, he wouldn't let me stay for long.

She went on, "Do you realize who you are messing with?" I didn't, and this was becoming like a foreign conversation to me.

She said, "That's Ratboy from the Dogg Pound!"

"Huh?! What is the Dogg Pound?!" When I asked, she was just as dumbfounded as I was. She couldn't believe I didn't have a clue. The only dog pound I knew of was the SPCA.

As our conversation continued, she brought me up to speed on what happened in the West End. The only time I heard of some things she was talking about was from TV, the news, or movies. Where I grew up, I was fortunate enough not to have to face a lot of things that were going on in Richmond at the time. The only reason I knew about some things was from my curiosity. Trust me, if my grandparents or parents knew some things I was in to, let's say you wouldn't be reading this story.

On the strength of her being his cousin, we became friends. I'm thankful I met her because that conversation got me thinking and putting pieces together about certain things. Don't get me wrong, I knew I was dating a dope boy. I wasn't stupid, but I didn't know how deep he was in that life until I started to pay closer attention.

Richmond, VA, was very hot during this time. I'm talking murder capital hot. It was a scary time for a lot of us. And my Jay Jay was right in the thick of things. Beef over different neighborhoods, drug wars, you name it, it was happening in the 804. The '90s was nothing pleasant within Richmond, and the way things were going, they would be worse before they got better.

As the days passed, we hung out a lot, just riding around, sitting in the car, and chilling. I wanted to spend as much time with him as possible. We grew deeper and deeper in love. Our conversations were so intense. Our lives were in a whirlwind, and we were not interested in slowing down. He always reminded me I would be his wife despite my nonchalant reactions.

We hung out almost every day, and we had to talk to each other every night before bed, it was like we were already an old married couple, especially since we were not having sex! He never even mentioned sex to me! I thought something was wrong with this guy! I came out and asked him one day. "Why haven't you asked to have sex with me yet?"

With a confused look on his face, he responds, "Ummmm, I don't know. I'm not pressing it, and it's not an issue for me. Is it for you?" That got my mind wandering. I guess if he didn't press the issue. Why should I? It kind of made me want him much more!

Spring came around, and so did time for him to take me out without distractions. So, I set the time and day to go on an official date. I offered to drive, so I picked him up. He wore his best street fashion, fresh white tee, jeans, and fresh white uptowns. He got in the car, amped to show off his money at an expensive place. I wish I could have taken a picture of his face when we pulled up at a park! He rolled with it, though.

We walked the entire park! It was hot, and the park was huge, but he still walked and talked with me, holding my hand the whole time, we talked about anything that came to our mind, especially about what I had been hearing about him. His palms were still sweaty. We made it to the rose garden and took a break in the gazebo.

While we sat there, Jay Jay started to open a little more about his lifestyle. I could tell he was still hiding some things. Not to deceive me, but to protect me from the craziness of his reality. I took what he said to me into consideration. Our date made me let my walls down. I believed this guy truly liked me for who I was. I had no idea the future I had imagined would turn out to be such a long hard road.

A change came for us quickly. The reality of his life started to become clear to me, and things were getting heated. After that day, more and more of the truth began to reveal itself. If I argued in school with a guy, dudes would show up to handle it. If I needed anything, someone showed up to bring it to me. I sneezed, someone was there to offer a tissue. It was that serious.

As the weather got hotter, so did the city, and my boyfriend was in the middle of it all. It got to the point that if I didn't hear from him when I was used to hearing from him, I would call every hospital and jail to make sure he was okay. Who the hell was I dating? I mean, when I asked, he assured me that he wanted to get out, but he was in too deep. I didn't know what to do or think because, by this time, I couldn't imagine living without him.

When we were together, I was with Jonathan or Jay Jay. I never saw the "Ratboy" side of him until a problem arose one day. I got a page from a friend telling me of a problem she was having with this guy. She asked me to meet her somewhere so that we could handle him. Jay Jay and I met up with her, and things quickly got out of hand. The argument between her and the guy escalated quickly. Then he referred to me as a bitch. Why did he say that about me with Jay Jay there?! The next thing I know, "Ratboy" was in full form. He was a completely different person. I tried my best to get him out of that boy's face. "Please stop baby, don't do this!"

The desperation in my voice calmed him enough to get in the car with me. I settled in the driver's seat and before I knew it POW POW POW!!!!! I sped off only to realize it was Ratboy firing the shots! I yelled, "STOPPPP, PLEASE!!!" He stopped, and I pulled the car over to calm down. I was scared to death. I looked at him like what just happened?! "Ain't nobody gonna call my girl a bitch!" I shook my head and pulled off again. I stayed silent the entire time. He knew I was pissed.

I couldn't believe what had taken place. All I knew was I never wanted to see "Ratboy" again. Two days after this altercation, I happened to catch the news, and what do I see? A group of guys, covering their faces with bandannas with the headline "GANGS IN RICHMOND" on the Channel 6 news. And who pops out at me? My Man!!!! UGHHHHHHHHHH!!!! I was more scared than hurt. What was I supposed to do if he got hurt or locked up? I had no idea what to do. I paged him 911! We have to talk NOW!

I met Jay Jay at his house, and we talked. I told him how scared I was to lose him and practically begged him to tell me everything he could. He assured me that he was not in a gang and wanted to put this life in his past, but it was a lot deeper and more complicated than just walking away. The more we talked, the sadder I got. I understood what he was and wasn't telling me. The conversation ended with tears and a kiss, and then sex.

We both were scared like it was our first time having sex! When we finished, we talked a little more to make sure we were on the same page. I eventually forgave him, but that "Ratboy" guy, he was on my shit list. I wasn't 100% good, but at least I knew to be prepared to see him again. And unfortunately, it came sooner than later.

hapter three

As time passed, my worry about him got worse. Then, that worry for him turned in to worry about me. I was pregnant. I was scared shitless, and he was happy as ever. "You know damn well I can't tell anyone! My grandparents and parents are going to kill me!"

"I got you, baby, we're going to be good!" After the initial shock was over, talks of the baby being a boy, and naming him Daquan, became an everyday conversation. I knew how bad he wanted this child, and he was in love with it already. I worried so much about continuing to hide the pregnancy. That worry soon turned to sadness. We lost the baby. It's funny how we planned this whole scenario out of what our lives would be like with this child, and in the end, we were both heartbroken. I never told anyone outside of a good friend I looked at as another mother. She helped us both through the sadness. But this was only the beginning.

About two months after the miscarriage, I had a day off and went about my day running errands. I spoke to Jay Jay, and he told me that they were going to the amusement park later that day, and he would see me when he got back. We said our "I Love you's," and that was that. The entire day went past, and suddenly, a feeling hit me in my chest like a ton of bricks. I hadn't heard from him, and I was worried. I paged him and paged him and paged him again. No callback. Then, I started making my routine calls, hospital to hospital, jail to jail. No one had a record of him. So, I decided to ride to the house. I got out and knocked on the door, tapping my foot and waiting for someone to answer. Then here comes the neighbor, "Ma'am, no one is there. The police just left there and locked them up". I will never forget those words.

It seemed like it was forever before I finally heard from him. The phone rang, and those famous words, YOU HAVE A COLLECT CALL FROM JONATHAN, came across the line. I was so happy to hear his voice finally. It was the shortest but longest conversation in history. It's started and ended with these words, "I'm sorry, I love you." I cried so much I couldn't cry anymore.

I was still in school and still working, so most of the communication came through his dad. He didn't allow me to go to court or know what was going on until there was a final decision. Waiting frustrated the hell out of me, but looking back that was his way of keeping the stress away.

While going through the trial, I would talk to him personally, maybe four times a month. We sent messages back and forth through his father or his brothers, but he tried to keep me out of things as much as possible. The time came for sentencing, and I can't even begin to say what was going through my mind. It would be one thing if I were keeping up with step by step, talking to the lawyer, etc. Jay Jay didn't allow any of that. The people who I was in contact with, held their loyalty to him and would not tell me things either.

Two weeks passed, and I finally get a call. My happiness quickly turned to sorrow when I heard the verdict.......27 YEARS! Twenty-seven years to serve concurrently. A year and some change into this relationship and now this! My entire world stopped. By this time, Jay Jay was 18. I could not even begin to think about how this would play out.

"I'm not asking you to do this time with me." Those words pierced my heart. Why would he say that to me? We had been through so much in our short time together. Why would he expect me to leave him like this? In my young dumb brain, I couldn't fathom the thought of me not being there. I didn't consider the type of work I was signing up for by staying. He insisted that this was not what he wanted for me, but I was hell-bent on making that decision for myself. I loved this guy. He meant so much to me. And no matter how much I tried to prepare myself for the "what-if's," I couldn't rid myself of the thought of him away for so long. This sentence was too much. What are we supposed to do?

By the end of that conversation, we had agreed to whatever may come our way. I think I was the only one that wasn't being logical. In his eyes, he had failed me. I cried for days and was so unstable. I masked my sadness when I started smoking weed. That was the only way to calm myself and take my mind away from what was going on. My friends were not a go-to source because I simply chose that option. I thought that some things should be held sacred in a relationship, and I didn't want to hear any outside opinions. I wanted to stick with my man.

hapter four

High school graduation came, and then I was off to college. I had also moved out with some friends, and I was not looking back. The time came for a visit. I prepared for a whole two weeks to see my baby face to face. I was sneaking to go, but I had a great alibi. A friend of mine attended college ten minutes away from where he was. So I told the story that I was going to see her. 7 am, and I was on my way to Lawrenceville Correctional Center by myself.

The adrenaline rush was real! That was a long lonely ride, but my excitement overshadowed that feeling. I pulled up and instantly got sick to my stomach. My nerves were on edge. The last time I was inside a prison, I was seven years old, visiting my dad at a lower level camp. It was nothing like what I saw now. I swallowed my fear as the female frisked me up and down, talk about an uncomfortable experience. Finally, I was at the door to enter the visitation room.

When the door opened, it was like the entire room was staring at me. It made me that much more uncomfortable. I tried so hard to keep from having a panic attack. So many thoughts were going through my mind. Had Jay Jay been fighting? What if a fight breaks out in here? What do I do if another woman pops up during this visit? Jay Jay never gave me a reason to think he was not loyal, but listening to stories from other people, which was not a good idea, I couldn't help but think it may happen to me. To keep from staring, I found a poster on the wall and pretended to read it until he came out. I was so focused I didn't even see him come to the table. When I realized he was standing there, the flood gates opened.

My baby!!! He didn't look the same to me anymore. It was like I could see all of his emotions on his face. He looked good physically, but there was pain in his eyes. He had cut his hair (state regulations), and he was in the prison blues. We hugged each other so tight for so long, and the guard had to instruct us to be seated. I looked into those eyes and teared up again. He dropped his head. "I know, baby, it's okay."

I wanted to believe what he said, but I couldn't wrap my head around how this would work, especially since this was not even six months into his sentence. I tried to put the tears aside to make for a pleasant visit. There was no need to take up the time grieving over what the next 27 years would bring. I could at least help him forget about going back in the cell, even if it was just for a couple of hours.

We got some snacks, talked a little, and laughed a lot. After a while, I kind of forgot where we were. The smile on his face was everything to me because I could see how hard it was for him. We talked about plans for the future, things he needed me to take care of, and, most importantly, was I sure I wanted to do this. That angered the hell out of me. But I knew he was only looking out for my best interest. Of course, my response to that was, "Stop playing with me, Jonathan!" He laughed, and eventually, so did I.

He told me that he was going to get a tattoo of my name on him. "Why would you do that?" I wasn't big on name tats. It seemed like they were bad luck. But his mind was already made up. We finished our snacks, took some pics, and before we knew it, the visit was over.

The happiness quickly turned around when it was time for him to go back behind that loud door. I hugged him so tight and told him that I would be back down for the next visit soon. There was school and work, so I had to make room to visit him. I made sure that I would be able to visit him whenever possible by any means necessary. It was my duty as his girl. But looking back, I didn't realize what I was doing or why. I just knew I was in love.

hapter five

After a while, the meaning of love started to get a little cloudy. I mean, it seemed like things were getting worse by the second. The phone calls were getting expensive, the visits were getting further and further apart, and Jay Jay was getting into more and more trouble. I never knew that the excitement that I had from the start of the first visit would turn into a dreadful feeling. I mean, I thought that the sentence of 27 years would make anyone straighten up and fly right. That's the way my head worked. But as the days went by, Jay Jay began to act more like his street personality, "Rat Boy." And that irritated me to the max.

I tried to hide my frustration through the phone sometimes. I didn't want to make our situation worse by complaining. But I was agitated with

Jay Jay's attitude. Why was he not acting like he wanted to be home? The possibility of parole was not an option, but damn, at least keep your good time. I pushed my feelings about the situation so far down in my soul, and I became numb. I did what I thought I was supposed to do as if it was a job.

He could see how frustrated I was growing, but I thought I hid it well. No matter how mad I was at him, as soon as I saw his face, all the anger and frustration went away. I was pretty much putty in his hands. I melted when he sent me a pic of the tattoo he got. There it was across his almost white back in HUGE writing, SONYA AND JAY FOREVER. I could not believe he got the tat. But he never went back on any of his words, so why should I be shocked.

Time went along, and I began to be on a name basis with the guards. It was always pleasant when it came to our interaction, but they would tell if Jay Jay had been out of order. He hated that. I'm not sure why he took it as them snitching on him because he knew he couldn't hide things from me. Good or bad, we would always be upfront and honest with each other. Some things would come back to me by way of some friends, other things Jay Jay would just tell me. All of it added to my frustration because I just wanted him to behave. I didn't realize it wasn't that easy. He had to wear the mask of the convict that he was. He had to live a particular lifestyle to survive.

One night when we were talking on the phone, Jay Jay expressed to me what he wanted me to wear on our next visit. "I want you to wear a skirt when you come next time, babe." My green ass had no idea why he wanted it, but I obliged. I bought a skirt that met the regulations for a visit. I paired it up with a cute shirt and shoes to make sure my look was perfect. The skirt was right length, but I was kind of scared that they would not let me in. Depending on who was working, some of the CO's were stricter than others. Jay Jay must have known the deal because that was the skimpiest search I had been through since he had been there.

I went inside the visitation room and waited for my baby. I got the snacks that he liked and took them back to the table. He finally came out, and his eyes lit up when he saw that I wore that skirt.

It was then when I realized that the visit was more than a visit to him. I would have to provide visual stimulation when I came. That was his way of enjoying me and escaping what was going on behind those bars. The visit went as usual until he slid in close and whispered, "you gonna let me get some?"

"Get some 'what'?" I was all loud.

"Shhhhhh," he said, "You know what I mean." I had the dumbest look ever on my face. How in the hell were we supposed to pull this off?

"How?"

Jay Jay started to laugh and said, "Come on; let's go take a picture." By then, I got the hint, but I was still very nervous. I couldn't allow myself to do it. As we approached the picture area hand in hand, I squeezed his hand. He looked at my face and knew I didn't want to go through with it. We stood in the normal posing position, him wrapping his hands around me from behind, and took the picture. He whispered in my ear, "It's okay baby, I understand, and I love you." Part of me felt like I let him down, but my morals would not let me rest. I just didn't have the nerve.

The next month or so worked well for us. We created a schedule for calls and visits. If I was lucky enough to catch a night shift on visiting day, I could sneak in an unscheduled visit. I lived my life and tried to maintain my relationship with Jay Jay, piece together my life for us to do this time together. Prison life on the outside was hard. I didn't know how to keep things level without saying or doing something that may hurt his feelings. I was smoking weed out of control. That was how I dealt with things. But of course, when the high wore off, the reality was still there. I tried to hide my weed smoking from him, but Jay Jay still had eyes and ears to the street.

One night that weed smoking got the best of me. I did the unthinkable. I had a one-night stand. To this day, I don't know why I did it. The weed played a significant role, but I should have had more restraint. I felt terrible when it was over. Not only for the action but because I couldn't hide it from Jay Jay. We were always honest with each other, and I couldn't hide this from him. It took me a couple of days, but on the next visit, I told him. I didn't want to say it to him over the phone because I needed to see his face and his facial expression.

When I told him, he dropped his head. I tried to hold my tears, but I couldn't. To my surprise, he grabbed my hand and said, "It's okay, baby."

"It's not, Jonathan. I messed up bad, hurt you, and you don't want to say it. I understand if you hate me, you should."

He lifted his head, "Listen to me. I will never hate you. If I hadn't left you out there, this would have never happened. I asked you if this is what you wanted to do, but I'm not stupid!

You are young, you have needs, and shit happens, RIGHT?!"

That statement made my stomach uneasy. I didn't quite understand what he was saying. We continued our conversation, more tears from me, more comfort from him. At the end of the visit, we hugged as usual, but he broke down. That killed me!!! He held me tight as he cried and didn't let go. The guards didn't bother us. I guess they knew it wasn't a good time for us. I grabbed his face as he did mine, we wiped each other's tears, said our "I love you's" and I went on my way.

As time went on, I held so much guilt in my heart for what I did. Jay Jay had forgiven me, but I had not forgiven myself. This guilt on top of life, in general, put more pressure on me. So much I couldn't bear. The partying, smoking and drinking was getting to be a regular thing for me. Those were the only times I was happy. When I was drunk or high, I was in another world. My behavior angered a lot of people, especially Jay Jay. He would voice his opinion, but he knew it didn't have much influence since he wasn't physically here. I didn't think it affected him, but he started to get into a lot of trouble in there, and I knew it was due to all the anger and frustration he had built up from what was going on between us.

After a weekend of partying, I woke up to go to work but didn't feel well. Jay Jay called me that morning, and I told him how I was ill. He usually called me in the evening time, but he knew when things were not right, so he would call just to soothe whatever feeling he had.

"After work, go to the doctor"

"I'm good babe, probably just hungover from the weekend." He didn't like that, but he always let things slide. He always said, "If I hadn't left you out here, certain things would not have happened." I assured him that I would go if I didn't feel any better. He told me he would call me back at the usual time, and we went about our way. I went to work, feeling like crap, and stayed there until my relief came in around 1 o'clock. I had to go to the doctor something was not right!

My doctor told me I could come in. I sipped on a ginger ale as I waited, hoping it would cure nausea and vomiting. A nurse called to the back and I explained my symptoms. She asked about my period, but it was normal for me to miss it from time to time. She gave me the cup for a urine sample, and the rest was history. The doctor came into the room with a bag full of information. He handed me a book, "What to Expect while Expecting." I'll never forget how he said, "Congratulations! You are going to be a mommy!"

My face dropped. I could not believe it. My emotions were mixed. I was scared but not because I was too young this time. I was 19 at this point. But how in the hell am I going to explain this to Jay Jay? I wanted Jay Jay to call, so I could get this explanation out of the way.

I cried and cried until I got his call. When Jay Jay came on the line, I cried more. He didn't even ask me why I was crying, all he said was, "You pregnant, ain't you?" I broke down even more despite him trying to console me. He had the same attitude as he did for the first pregnancy, "we will be good, baby."

"WE!!!! What do you mean WE! This baby isn't yours! I don't like this dude. I barely know him!!!" He knew I was so upset.

"Sonya, this is OUR child! And that's just it! I don't give a damn about that dude, and you don't either, so let's have this baby!" He kept saying WE could do this, and things would be okay. I was so shocked at his response and the pregnancy that I couldn't breathe. Even though I was unsure about how this was going to take place, I was going to have this child. We were going to make something work.

Visits had to stop, of course. We didn't want any questions to arise and must explain something that was none of their business. But through it all, Jay Jay made me feel more special than what he already did. I had doubts, but he knew how to allow me to process it and reassured me everything would be alright. The pregnancy brought us closer even though we were physically apart. Some times were lonely, of course. Nights when I wanted him to be there to hold me, visits to the doctor, the baby shower, all of that was hard for us. Especially having to deal with the fact that the conception was frowned upon by friends and family. It wasn't right, but it was right for us. We got through the criticism, the doubt, and, most of all, the reality of days to come.

Chapter six

May 13th, I gave birth to our son. My friends and family were there, but of course, the void of Jay Jay not being there was present. After everyone was gone and the room was silent, I laid in bed and cried. There were tears of joy and pain at the same time. I got up to wash my face and looked in the mirror. I was a mother. A single mother! His biological father was living his own life, and Jay Jay was in prison. Even though our son was the light of my life, this was the beginning of my depression. I didn't realize it, but this was where the test of time began.

Jay Jay was very excited to have another son. His excitement was overshadowed by guilt when he saw his baby for the first time. "I left you out here alone to have our son, and I'm not coming home any time soon. You don't deserve this Sonya". He had said similar words before, but this time, I felt he couldn't be righter. I loved him dearly, but this was not what I had in mind for my future. And now I have a child, this was not what intended for him either.

I didn't know what to do other than raise my son and deal with life. This arrangement was not ideal for me in my family, but I did have a support system. I changed my courses and attended school online. My grandparents kept our son when I went to work. Life went on and caused more strain on our relationship.

The visits became far and few in-between. Life was happening, and it didn't leave any time for me to think about the next time I could visit. Honestly, I didn't want to visit as much anymore. Taking my baby through the search process was not something I enjoyed doing. Jay Jay missed us, but he didn't like me coming to bring the baby and having to go through the search either.

It seemed Jay Jay was not the person I thought he should be. Every time I turned around, he was getting into situations. Still living in the light of the "Ratboy" personality and getting worse by the day. It was funny how he could turn it on and off, though. The phone calls were genuine Jay Jay, but the feedback was all about "Ratboy." He got transferred to a facility with a higher security level, and it pissed me off! "Do you think this is a joke?" "Baby, I'm trying, but I'm not gone take no shit off anyone!"

"It's not about that, JONATHAN!". When I was mad at him, I called him by his real name. "But baby..."

"I don't want to hear that! You got a 27-year sentence......STRAIGHT! Twenty-seven years away from any and everything you love! We should have been enough for you to straighten your ass up!"

If only I knew how wrong my opinion was. He was in PRISON! Behind bars, in a facility full of men with the same crimes if not worse than his.

And I thought he was supposed to be an angel? I guess the part that confused me was how he was a completely different person when it came to his family and me. We couldn't accept him acting like Ratboy because we knew Jay Jay could be much better.

Time went on, and so did life. When I did get a chance to visit, I rarely took the baby. My anger for the way Jay Jay was behaving wouldn't let me be as happy and willing as I was in the beginning. He knew it too. We knew each other well enough to tell how each other what we felt. I had even started contemplating leaving him. I had an easy way out! He was in prison. How was he going to find us if I just decided to leave? My heart wouldn't let me do it. I was afraid of how I would hurt him. Even though he caused me so much pain by being gone, my heart wouldn't let me turn my back on him.

There were telltale signs when I did visit. I fell asleep at the wheel one time and woke up when I hit the guardrail. I wasn't hurt, and the car was still running, so I kept going. When I arrived at the facility, I realized I dented the door, and I couldn't open it. I should have turned back then, but I didn't. Another time, I had someone riding with me. Her husband was at the same facility as Jay Jay was, and she had her kids with her. We made it there okay, but on the way back, the transmission went, and we had to call for a tow truck back into the city. It was a freaking nightmare. How much more was I going to subject myself to by continuing this relationship?

After years of uncertainty, I finally got my chance to walk away. Jay Jay had been in for five years. Our son was two, and I was at my wit's end. I deserved more, and Jay Jay deserved more, our son deserved more. I waited for a call one night that I didn't come. Only to find out he transferred to a maximum-security prison. That was it!!! I was so upset. No matter how apologetic he was, I didn't want to listen a word he said. I stopped answering the calls, and I stopped writing the letters, I stopped caring. I grew very numb. My most important job was to be a mother to my son. But how could I be a good mother when I was so depressed and hurt. I lost my best friend and a piece of my happiness. Prison had locked up our love.

Jay Jay would still write, of course. He sent letters and cards for birthdays and holidays. He never missed the chance to put our son on the angel tree for Christmas. But my responses were little to none. I sent cards and pictures of the baby, but nothing more. I didn't want to open the door I had closed. That would require an explanation on my part, and I was not ready to explain why I had become so distant. I didn't want to explain to him how hurt I had become. He already expressed to me he knew this would be hard, so it was more like admitting he was right. I failed him, and most importantly, I failed myself.

As my life went on, I started to do anything to mask the pain. I began to entertain another guy who ultimately turned out to be my second child's father. We had a good relationship for the most part, but problems arose when I forgot to check the mail one day, and a letter from Jay Jay had come. I was always honest about my dealings with Jay Jay, but this guy was not comfortable with me still having contact with him. Despite my anger toward Jay Jay and though communication was minimal, I wouldn't completely shut him out. He is my son's father and my best friend.

The arguments with my daughter's father became more frequent. I was tired of trying to explain my reasoning to someone who refused to deal with serious matters. It was becoming more and more of a downhill battle and it wasn't worth fighting. After the birth of my daughter, it wasn't long before I was questioning why I stayed with him. I realized it was not a real attraction at all. I was simply trying to feel good at the moment, create a solid disconnection from Jay Jay and live happily ever after. Epic failure. Before I knew it, we broke up, and I moved to a new place. I thought for sure I was done with Jay Jay then. I didn't even bother to tell him we were moving, I just left. About three months after settling into the new place, guess what graced my mailbox! A letter! I should have known he would find us.

hapter seven

It always felt good when I saw the writing on the envelope, but I didn't want to show it. I knew this could make me want to revert to doing time with Jay Jay again. The letter was typical words from him. He never mentioned the fact of how he knew where I lived. He simply asked how we were, congratulated me on the new place, and sent his love. Jay Jay told me he missed me, and he hoped we would get a chance to be together like we used to.

Those words put a partial smile on my face, but my scared heart only allowed me to think it was all prison talk. In faith, I wrote him back. I told him everything I was going through. That's just how we communicated. I could always talk to him, and he would understand. By the end of the letter, I had written four pages. Maybe letters would at least open a better line of communication for us, and we could work on the rest another time. I sent it off and went on about my week. I came home from work one day to his response. The envelope was thick, and it kind of gave me butterflies. Maybe this was the letter to show me he was changing.

The first paragraph or so had my full attention. Jay Jay told me he understood my feelings. He apologized for the actions that caused him to move up in the ranks. By the time I got into the second paragraph, I WAS PISSED. The first sentence, "When you get a chance, baby, it's some things I need you to send me." He started naming off things he needed like a flipping grocery list. I was mad as fire. He told me all of this only to butter me up to get stuff from me?! Here goes the hurt again!!! I knew I had set myself up. I AM DONE. Why did I respond to the letter? I felt worthless at that point. By the time the anger began to wear off, I had wondered why I had started this journey in the first damn place.

Years started to fly by me. Communication from Jay Jay was cards only. I sent one-page letters telling him we were okay, but the letters were icy. Eventually, all communication stopped. I guess he could sense through the writing how I was feeling and decided to let me be. Honestly, at the time, I was thankful. I didn't have to try to live a lie anymore. I was free. Or so I thought.

One day while at work, I look up to help a customer and who was it, Jay Jay's father, Sonny. His father and I had been in communication when we first met, but as things dropped off with Jay Jay, I lost the connection with his family. When we made eye contact, Sonny had this smirk on his face I would never forget. "How have you been?" He handed me his lottery slips.

"Good, and you?" I was so nervous about speaking to him. I didn't know how he was going to respond. He, as always, a man of few words, but I understood his looks.

"I have been good. Good to see you."

"Good to see you too, Sonny. How is your son?" I turned my face up a bit when I said that. I tried to give off the idea that I didn't care, but I was lying to myself and Sonny, and he knew it. He laughed, "You mean your man? He good."

"Nah, I said it correct, YOUR SON, him and I aren't friends anymore." I handed him his numbers back.

He smiled and said, "Y'all gone be alright" and walked out the door. I rolled my eyes and I knew he was going to tell Jay Jay he saw me. I was just hoping I wouldn't get a random phone call or a letter because I was not interested.

Sonny came around more and more. I worked a lot of hours, and he played a lot of numbers. Our conversations were becoming comfortable. I just knew it was a matter of time before I was going to hear from Jay Jay. Sonny and Jay Jay were the best of friends, so I knew when he spoke to his son, he told him everything about me. It didn't help that the store I worked at was a very popular store smack dab in the middle of the hood, so I was well-known. From the store and my "other life." So I knew things were getting back to him with no problem at all. I cared, but I didn't. At this point, my focus was on my kids and trying to make a better way for us all. And if that didn't include Jay Jay, then I would just have to deal with it.

I had other guys I dated. I refer to them as place holders. None of them were right for me. They just held a place for what I wanted and needed. Though I had companions, I was still in a mild depression. I was smoking weed like there was no tomorrow. I stayed high so that I could escape the pain. I was attracting the wrong people, falling for some complete idiots. Not all the guys were terrible, but the majority were no good. It took time for me to realize I was still trying to find Jay Jay in these other guys, and it was not happening at all. I was cautious about who I brought around my kids, though. They were rarely with me since I worked a lot, but when they were, I made sure I respected them enough not to bring them around just anyone.

# hapter eight

My "other life" caught up with me soon. I thought because I was working, I was covering myself from anything that may happen, but again, I was wrong. Hanging out with one of those no-good guys I dated, I caught my first charge, possession of marijuana. Fortunately, I put up what I had before I went to meet the guy. If I hadn't, I would have faced much worse charges. The guy had been messing around with another chick. He pissed her off, so she sent the police to his place. When they arrived, we had been smoking, so the house reeked of marijuana. It was only a little remaining in a bag. When the police asked whose weed was it, the bastard pointed to me!

Even though I was in the wrong, his karma for pointing the finger at me soon came to haunt him. That chick had made complaints against him, which resulted in four warrants. I agreed to say it was my weed and cooperated with the cops. Since I was polite, they wrote the ticket and let me go. They advised me of the possibilities of the outcome, but I was so shaken, the cop sounded like Charlie Brown's teacher, and all I could take in was, "I'm giving you a ticket and letting you go."

So, there I was with at possession charge. Luckily, it was my first offense, and I had a chance to redeem myself. This took a lot of work on my part. I went in front of one of the toughest judges in Richmond, and ironically, this was the same court building Jay Jay received his sentence. The judge gave me my options, and I took the one most beneficial to me. It was a costly option too! They hit me with fines, probation, suspended license, and a drug class, which I paid to take! I had to own up to the responsibility that I was wrong. I had been selling weed since high school, but I honestly thought I would never get caught. By this time,

I was 28 years old and on what seemed like a downward spiral, AGAIN! To add insult to injury, I didn't have my Jay Jay.

I did what I had to do to make sure the charge would not be on my record. I even backed away from selling weed and smoking. Really, I had no choice to stop smoking because drug testing was a part of my probation. In the drug class, I realized how depressed I was. The class wasn't only about drug use, but it was more about life. I realized the things that happened with Jay Jay were not the only source of my depression, but past childhood things I had never resolved. I never realized how my younger life impacted the relationships I had, especially the one with Jay Jay. My defense was to hurt you before you hurt me. When things seemed to go well with people, I think it's too good to be true, so I end it before they do to protect myself. I had been doing that for a while now and never realized it. The class made me realize why I was going through life the way I was. This realization made me more depressed.

All I could think was why would I do this to myself and others. Deep down I knew I was not the type of person to intentionally hurt people, but in all actuality, I had become that person. I hid my depression well and pretended everything was okay. Once the class was over, so was my sobriety. Back to smoking again, I had to. Life was so crazy and I didn't know how to handle it. My job paid well, but it wasn't safe. My side hustle was gone. Unfortunately, by then, Jay Jay was the furthest thing from my mind.

Work and life went on, and I met a guy I knew from school. We exchanged numbers, talked for a while, and soon we were a couple. He had a lot of flaws, but hey, so did I. He did treat me with respect. We moved to a completely different side of town, away from all the chaos of the city. The kids were in a new school, and they were into extracurricular activities. Things seemed to be getting a little better. I just rode the wave while it lasted. He proposed to me, and I accepted. Jay Jay was out of my mind, for sure. By then, it had been five years since we spoke, so I assumed he had moved on too. I was out! I could kind of see the light at the end of the tunnel. That light quickly dimmed as I went back into depression.

My fiancé and I were starting to have problems. On top of that, a part of my heart had Stage 4 cancer, my grandfather." The news of his sickness took a heavy toll on me. I knew my grandparents would pass one day, I just never thought it would come this soon and in this manner. The realization that my grandfather would not be here anymore made me put things in proper perspective. Things went so fast, and before I knew it, he was gone.

My world, my heart, the first man I loved had taken his last breath. I had no comfort. My so-called fiancé wasn't helpful at all, which made me despise him even more. I called off the engagement and suggested we go our separate ways. Before I could put the period on that sentence, I got a call from the landlord stating that the house we were in was in foreclosure, and we had to be out immediately. You could stick a fork in me because I was done.

When I got the call about the house, it was like someone punched me in my chest. It seemed like I couldn't get a grip on my life. I called my family for help. My grandmother told me to bring the kids and come live with her. It made sense, my grandfather was gone, and she was in the house alone. That was the best news I had heard in a while. So, time to pack, and that's what I did. I took a couple of days off work to handle my affairs. My focus was to on get out of that house and start over. My ex-fiancé took his time getting his things together, so I moved around him and forgot he was there. I had no interest in where he was going; I knew he wasn't going with me.

My little sister came over to help with the packing. When she came in the door, she brought in the mail. What did I see? A letter from the long-lost Jay Jay. The biggest smile came over my face and my heart. It was weird, though, because I knew that door that I thought

I close, flew right open and I hadn't opened the letter yet.

"Look at this here," I said to my sister, showing her the letter. She laughed and said, "Oh, you thought he wasn't going to find you?" I didn't think he would! How did he keep finding me?

I tucked the letter away to read it once I settled in. I wanted to prepare myself for whatever was in the envelope. Just seeing it made my whole attitude change. Jay Jay had that effect on me. The more I packed, the more anxious I was to read it. At the rate I was going, nothing he could say make me feel any worse than the recent life events had done. My heart was stone, I had no cares other than my kids. I was ready for something to change. I held on to the letter for a while. Truthfully, I was too scared to read it at that point. I wanted to get the move completed.

Grandma's house was a stressful time. It was like my childhood again; only I was the "parent." My grandfather took care of everything in the house, so my grandmother didn't know how to do a lot of things herself. My mom and aunt helped out with certain chores, but a great responsibility fell on me to take care of grandma's needs. I was needed so much. I had to cut hours at my job just to make sure she had proper care. This stressed me out because I had kids to feed. How in the world was I supposed to support my family if I could only work limited hours? I started smoking heavily again, drinking at night, and crying myself to sleep. I was so busy taking care of the family and trying to stay sane, but I was ready to explode.

My grandma decided to move into an independent living apartment, leaving the kids and me in the house. The arrangement sounded cool, but the bills made it difficult for me to keep up. My mom and sister moved in, and they took most of the stress of my shoulders. It was then that I had started to gain some clarity. I landed a job paying good money. I stopped smoking cold turkey and started to eat right. Another guy stepped into the picture, and we began dating. Slowly, I was getting myself back.

I came across the unopened letter one day and tried to prepare myself to read it. I knew it would come with some words that I was not ready to read like how much I hurt him and why did I do it. I wanted to apologize and let it be. But I realized life didn't work like that when I opened this letter.

"First, let me say that I hope and pray that you, the family, and the kids are all doing well, mentally, physically, and spiritually. As for myself, I'm chillin, trying to figure out what I did, where I went wrong, and if I will ever have you back on my life again. Baby, I know that throughout this time I haven't been the best boyfriend or friend because of how I was acting in prison, but baby this shit is HARD, and I'm still trying to figure out how I am going to make it for the rest of these years I have to do without the woman that I love, cherish and need. I want to spend the rest of my life with you, you inspire me, and I don't understand why I don't have you anymore. Sonya, I am hurting so much right now because I don't know if I will ever be able to get you back in my life. I don't know what to do, Sonya! Tell me what I did wrong for you to just up and leave me with no reason whatsoever, baby. I write to you, try to call and get no response at all. I'm up here at Sussex, locked down for 20 hours of the day and all I do is think about you and our son. I feel like I'm ready to lose my mind inside here. I know that I have taken you through a lot of things, but it was never on purpose. I was just trying to find my way to be able to complete this bid, as well as have you by my side. Now it seems as if those hopes and dreams are lost. Sonya, I miss you so much, your laugh, your smile, your sense of humor, just being able to hear your voice makes my day so much easier. To be able to see you makes this time seem like a vacation. But now that I no longer have that you in my life anymore, I don't know what to do, for real! To be honest, I feel that since I can't have you in my life, then life isn't worth living anymore, for real! I swear to you Sonya, every day that goes by that I don't hear from you or talk to you, I want to say fuck it and kill myself. But then I would hurt you, our son, and everyone else even more. But I don't know what to do! Damn! I don't know what else to do or say, Sonya. I'm hurting so much right now! Even the thought of you hurts my heart. If, by any chance, you can forgive me for my actions, just please write to me to let me know that you and Bear are okay. I will always love you no matter what Sonya. I will always be there for you, even if we are not together. I want you to be happy, even if I am not the one to provide that happiness. No matter what, you will always have a place in my heart. Well, I hope I hear from you. I will keep writing to let you know how I'm doing and to give you my unconditional love always. I love you, Sonya, Always and Forever, until the end of time.

Love always, Jonathan

My heart dropped, and so did the tears. I hurt one of the strongest people I knew. It was crazy because even though he was telling me how hurt he was, he also understood why I did it. I knew I hurt him but hearing it from him was much harder to take. This confirmed what I already knew. He needed someone much better than me. I slowly slipped back into depression.

One day, my birthday, to be exact, I was sitting in my truck in front of my cousin's house. We had a small cookout, and everyone was enjoying themselves having family time. I was in one of my moods, so I decided to go collect my thoughts by myself. My phone rings, "You have a collect call from Rico." I just knew it was going to say Jay Jay, but I forgot my brother told me he would be calling soon. "Hey, sis, happy birthday." "Thanks, bruh, what's good with you?" We chopped it up for a hot minute. "Hold on. Someone wants to talk to you."

The person comes on the phone "Happy Birthday" It was Jay Jay. I began to smile as I told him, thank you. I was so stuck I couldn't think of anything else to say. "Do you know who you are talking to?" "Of course, I do, Jonathan!" He laughed a little. "Look, I know you are dealing with someone, and we haven't talked in a while, but I wanted to take my chances to wish you a happy birthday, check on you and the kids, and say I love y'all." I couldn't do anything but cry. "Are you still there?" "I'm here," as I wiped my face. I had mixed emotions. He was at a much lower-level prison than he was the last time we talked. I was so happy but also cautious to see if he had changed.

Jay Jay and I talked for the remainder of the call. He invited me to come to visit. I thought about it but not for long. What harm could it do? Besides, I was in control. If things went left, all I had to do was what I did best, LEAVE.

hapter nine

I filled out the visitation form and sent it in. It had been seven years since I last spoke to him. I was as nervous as hell. When the day came for me to visit, I didn't dress too cute. I had on jeans and sneakers. I didn't want to make it seem like I was open to being back with him. I went in and sat straight down without buying any snacks. My nerves took over and I tapped my foot while I waited. The door opened to the back room, and in he walked. It was Jonathan, not Ratboy, not even Jay Jay, JONATHAN. I could tell he was not the same, and his conversation confirmed it all. He came over to the table, and we hugged.

My face had a look of shock as he looked at me and laughed. "What's funny?" I said with an attitude. "You! Still trying to act hard, huh?" I smirked a little. He knew me well. "Why did you look so shocked when you saw me?" "Because you not the same anymore." Tears welled up in my eyes. He had changed for the better, and I was so much worse. I was not for him anymore. He deserved better. Someone that wouldn't leave him high and dry, someone who could be a strength when he was weak, someone who wasn't broken and damaged. And that someone wasn't me anymore.

I asked him did he want something to eat, and of course, he did. On the way to the vending machine, he gave me a little pat on the butt with a look of delight. I rolled my eyes and kept walking. We got snacks and came to sit back down. We talked but not about what we should have talked discussed. He kept weirdly staring at me, "What happened to you, Sonya? I can tell you are hurt, but you're not the same. Your guard is up so high it's scary." He was right. I didn't want to act that way towards him. It was me who abandoned the relationship. I could not let it go. I needed help to get back to my true self.

The remainder of the visit went fine. Jonathan told me about how his father passed away. He also told me that he had reconnected with his mom, whom he hadn't seen or talked her to since childhood. We talked about all the trades he had received certification for and getting his GED. I was so glad for the change in him. We both agreed on rebuilding our relationship as friends. He was ending a relationship with someone. He told the girl that he would never have the tattoo of my name on his back covered because he would always love me. I laughed so hard when he told me that, but he was dead serious.

"What is so funny?"

"I can't believe you said that to her! She a good one because we probably would have fought!"

"Well, it was the truth, and sometimes, the truth hurts"

At the end of the visit, we stood up to hug. I looked at him and said, "I'm so proud of you, Jonathan." He smiled and thanked me. We hugged, and he whispered to me, "I still love you, I always will." I already knew that, but I just wished I loved myself as much as he loved me. I was lost, and I couldn't even consider which way I wanted to go. All I knew was I felt good at the moment, so I rode with it. Once those doors closed behind me, I went right back to the ice-cold person I had become.

The rest of the day, I was on cloud nine, until the phone rang, and it was my current boyfriend. He and I were on good terms, but it was a long-distance relationship. Of course, I never spoke of the visit with Jay Jay with my boyfriend. It was a "need to know" situation and I wasn't telling him. We kept in contact. The guy I was dealing with had started to stray, and I pretended like I didn't know. I was steadily working on my relationship with Jay Jay. I would rather have my best friend back than someone I knew was doing me wrong.

 hapter ten

Jay Jay and I had started to get back on track. I kept my guard up because of how bad we hurt each other. He was so happy to have me again, and I don't think any of that mattered. One visit, he noticed I had my boyfriend's initials on my nails. He took a look and said, "Hmm." I started laughing. "That's about to change soon, ma'am." "Oh yeah?" "Oh yeah!" We both laughed. I knew he would stop at nothing to win me back. And honestly, I was not going to stop him. Funny how things fell into place because soon after, I was single again.

Things were going along fine until my grandmother passed away. It was then I saw I had no one at all. There were friends and some family that cared, but I still felt alone. I knew my grandparents would not be on this earth forever. I just wasn't prepared to lose them so soon. God was the only real comfort. I prayed and talked to Him until I ran out of words to say. That was such a dark moment in my life, and God was my only sanity. Jay Jay comforted as well as he could, but he had also been hurt by death when he lost his father. So it was like we were both healed together. I was slowly getting my Jay Jay back. But I still questioned my ability to be what he needed me to be. I couldn't be what I needed to be for myself or my kids. I had to get it together.

As time went on, we helped each other heal. We talked to each other through things. We started to have the conversations we needed to have. Jay Jay's time was coming to an end soon. I wanted to see where his head was at before coming home. He was trying to make sure my mind and heart were in the right place to spring the plans he had in mind on me. Eventually, I met his mom and her side of the family. Our relationship clicked like we had known each other forever. Jay Jay's aunts and grandmother were the only females in his family I had associated with until then. She and I talked about certain things that made me understand Jay Jay a little better. We were different, yet our paths were similar. We were both hurt from the past and never really dealt with it. It was then I realized I needed to release some things to have a healthy future.

Unfortunately, his mom was battling with cancer. She was already in her last stages, but that woman was a spitfire! She fought until the very end like a soldier. I was glad she got a chance to visit Jay Jay, and they got a chance to talk through some issues. That was a big part of his healing. He finally had answers he was seeking for many years. His mom and I formed a great relationship over a brief time.

One day, she called me saying she was tired of going in and out of the hospital. "I'm tired of them poking on me. I'm not going back there. My son and I are in a good place, so I am good.

Tell him I love him, we are good, and thank you for accepting me back into his life."

"I will, ma." There wasn't anything other to say than that. I watched my grandfather suffer from cancer, Jay Jay's father died of cancer, so I couldn't possibly be selfish and try to convince her to go by the doctor's orders. I relayed the message to Jay Jay, and two weeks later, she passed away.

The devastation was hard. I knew my baby was hurting, but prison life would only allow him to show little emotion. We had both taken significant losses in a short time. We talked to each other through the rough times. As much as we were allowed, we embraced each other during our visits. There were times when I felt I couldn't give him the consoling he needed. It was just a thing where he had to process the emotions himself, but his environment was not fit for him to do so. I did what I could when I could. Hell, I was still healing myself.

Our relationship grew stronger. I had my friend back. I wanted to see that he understood what I saw in him from the start. From the looks of it, he understood. Our separation was a learning time for him, learning more about himself and getting the education he deserved. Even though he was hurt, he understood what was happening and used that to make himself a better person. I was genuinely thankful for that. It was then that I realized prison truly saved his life.

I had continued to visit him almost every weekend. Each visit, I saw a better person. The funny thing was, he saw the same, hurt, Sonya. "When are you going to stop being so guarded with me?" I felt small when he asked. I was doing my best to try to hide my fears, but he saw straight through it. With tears in my eyes, I answered, "I don't know." We talked about what thoughts were going through my head, and I apologized for being this way. He wouldn't accept the apology because he didn't believe I owed it to him. "If I had not left you out in the world by yourself, you would not have experienced some hurt, so I APOLOGIZE." That was hard for me to accept. I blamed a lot of my past on myself, so I felt awkward letting him take the blame. I wasn't sure what to say after that conversation until he came out of the blue and said, "*Will you marry me*?"

hapter eleven

I froze. A million things were going through my mind, and I had no idea how I could process the thoughts enough to answer. In my mind, I felt it wasn't an appropriate time, but my heart was all in. I was so confused I felt nauseous. I couldn't break Jonathan's heart again, but I had to be honest. So I grabbed his hand and looked him in the eyes and said, "This is not the right time Jonathan. I love you, but this is not the right time." There was so much hurt in his eyes, but he understood. "It's okay baby, I know what you mean, but it doesn't mean I'm going to stop trying. You are mine, and I love you." He kissed me, and we got up to end the visit. We hugged for what seemed like forever. I started to cry as he whispered in my ear, "I love you, babe, and we will be good. I PROMISE!" He always had faith about us, and he was determined to make his promise a reality.

I thought about all the conversations we had on each phone call and visit. Especially the one when Jonathan asked to marry me. Why in the hell would he want to marry me? I knew we both had faults over the years, but I didn't give myself enough credit to be seen as marriage material for anyone. Then I wondered what other people would think. I'm not sure why so many people had shown me who they were since the passing of my grandparents, I shouldn't have given a damn about what they thought. It was still a factor, though, and I had to make my decision. There was only one thing I really could do, PRAY. At the end of the prayer, I was in tears. I listened to God and followed His directions accordingly. I talked to my mom about it and said two words which changed my entire outlook on the situation. "WHY NOT?!" She continued, "life is too short for you to worry about what others think about you. People will always have their opinions about you, don't worry about them, do what's best for you!" I talked to the kids about it too. Our son said, "Mommy, if that's what makes you happy, then I'm all for it." The other kids followed suit. Those words gave me all the confidence I needed to make my decision. I couldn't wait for the phone to ring later that night.

I finally got the phone call I was waiting to receive. "Hey babe, how was your day?!" He started to tell me about all the things he had done and what went on throughout the day. I loved listening to him talk about what he did. He spoke with such pride about the classes he was taking and the work he was doing. I know he felt good because it had the same effect on me. After we talked for a while, I said, "Baby, I got a surprise for you this weekend!" "What is it?" "Now if I told you it wouldn't be a surprise now would it?" We both laughed. I knew he would be anxious about the surprise, but I wanted to keep it a secret until I got there. He kept asking, but I held tight to my tongue.

When visiting day came, I was so nervous. I was about to leap in faith with this one. But I felt confident in my choice. I had gone through so much change and depression, it was time for renewal. I felt this was my first step. He came to the table with the biggest smile on his face. It was like it was Christmas Eve, and he was coming to see Santa for his gifts. We hugged as usual and sat down. I reached out for his hands. They were still sweaty after all of these years. "Why are your hands always sweaty when I come?" "You make me nervous, woman!" We laughed. He was so silly. I looked in his eyes to try to catch the vibe. He started to look more concerned than excited, so it was the time to tell him. "So, I was thinking, let's do it," "Do WHAT?!" "Let's get married! Why not?! We love each other, right?" Words could not begin to describe the look on his face when I said that. He was so happy. His face turned red as a beet. "Are you serious?!" "Very! I love you, Jonathan, and I want to be your wife." "Well, I need to do this the right way!" He slides his chair out to go down on one knee. I started to hyperventilate!

I was so nervous, yet happy, yet scared! So many emotions! I covered my face as I kept repeating, "Oh my God, Oh my God!" You would think I would be calm since I am the one who initiated this. But I was overcome with happiness. "Sonya Hart, will you be my wife?" Through all the emotions and heavy breathing, I said, "YES!"

I saw the guard coming over to us. He congratulated us and politely told him to take his seat. People clapped as much as they could and told us congratulations. It was one of the happiest times of my life. I felt accomplished, needed, and worthy. Most of all, I believed I could be myself again. The remainder of the visit was like I had floated away to Heaven. I can't even remember the rest of our conversation. I just knew I was going to be Mrs. Jonathan Staples. That's all that mattered at the moment.

And so, it happened. In front of the people who meant the most to us, we said "I Do" at Deep Meadow Correctional center. I can honestly say that day ignited the "I don't care" flame in me. It had always been there, but my vulnerability never really allowed me to fully commit. I may have said it, but deep down inside, the opinions of others truly affected me. I threw all of that away and started a new life. Whatever problems I had were forgotten, whatever issues I had with people were forgiven. I began to live again.

From that day on, we started a brand- new lifestyle. We made promises to each other and held each other accountable if we fell short. Our main rule was to communicate whatever thoughts came to us dealing with the relationship, never to end a conversation in anger, and, most importantly, to love each other more and more each day. We had to be realistic about our marriage and the vows we took before God. We worked hard to get to this point in our lives to let anything mess this up.

Jay Jay had five years left, so the honeymoon phase had to be wrapped up quickly to prepare for his homecoming. A lot had changed in the outside world, and his world stopped over 20 years ago. Homes have replaced the block they used to hustle on we can't afford. The vehicles are talking, and cell phones no longer come in bags that plugged into the lighter. Cars have push-starter buttons, things appliances run by voice command, and everything he was used to was gone. Worry came over me so fast, but I knew we had the strength to push through whatever comes our way.

The more worry came over me, the more I translated it into the conversation. That was the main reason our bond separated in the first place. We had a communication barrier, and I wasn't willing to destroy what we had. I started introducing topics to him on things he had not given much thought too. At first, Jay jay was not about talking to anyone other than me about unresolved issues he had concerning his upbringing and other things in life besides us. "I am not going to talk to no counselor! For what?! They have not done the time I have, so how can they relate to what I have been through?" That was his initial response when I asked him about going to counseling. But by the time we finished the conversation, he admitted he needed more help; help which I couldn't give.

Knowing I couldn't provide what he needed firsthand didn't frustrate me as it would have in the past. I had an entirely new outlook on the future, and I felt obligated to be a vital part of it. We continued to talk about how things affected us from the past. We allowed each other to vent, and more importantly, we listened to each other. The more we talked, the more we understood the disconnection we had in the first place. Our conversations were therapeutic for us both. They brought us closer and closer. For the first time in a long time, I felt like I understood what he was going through. His pain matched mine. It was just uniquely presented. I could process my pain, but with him being in prison, he had to bottle up his grief and store it away in hopes that he would never have to deal with it again.

hapter twelve

I felt good about the new foundation that we were building. Every day was a step closer to him coming home. But it seemed like this journey was starting to hit another rocky point. The time was getting shorter for him to return home, but the visits were getting to be a bit much. There was a surge of overdoses and drugs at the facility he was in, and it called for more precautions during visitation. First, the bathrooms in the visitation room were locked. So, for you to use the restroom, you had to leave the visitation building, go back to the search building to use the bathroom, and be searched again. My answer was to use it before I came in, so I wasn't phased. Second, snacks such as chips, sandwiches, and other meals were taken away in the vending machines and reduced to nabs, cookies, and $3 protein bars. There were claims that contraband entered the prison through the vending items. This was okay with us as well. He would eat before he came out, and I would bring enough for a drink and maybe a candy bar. This new approach saved me a lot of money.

The last change was one I couldn't push away so quickly. The administration started to have the dogs meet people in the parking lot for a quick walk around before they entered the search building. At first, I wasn't bothered by the search. I had nothing on me, so there was no need for me to be scared. The first three weekends the dogs were out, I stopped, allowed them to do their job, and proceeded to visit my husband with no problem. The next weekend, things didn't go too well.

Sunday, March 19, 2017. A day I will never forget. I watched the officers with the dogs there as usual when I pulled in and parked my car. As I am walking to the officer with the K-9, another C.O. who was very familiar with me greeted me with a smile and "Good morning, how are you today?" "I'm well, thanks," I replied. I continued to walk to the correctional officer with the K-9 and assumed the position to allow the dog to walk around me. As I followed him with my eyes, he tugged at the dog to make the dog stop as if he smelled something. After all these years, I know what the procedure is for a dog who picks up the smell of contraband. They are supposed to sit down if they detect a scent. But this dog did not sit once. He stopped every time the officer jerked at the leash. I paid it no mind until I heard him tell the C.O. "take her in the office!". The C.O. and I looked at each other surprised. She asked him, "HER?!". "Yes!", looking at me and pointing, "Follow her." I followed as directed and wasn't concerned because I had nothing on me.

As I entered the room, it was an officer sitting at the table who instructed me to sit down. He asked, "Do you know why we pulled you in here?" "No.," trying to keep the evil eyes off him. "Well, the dog smelled a scent on you, and there is suspicion of contraband. Do you have anything on you, or have you been around anyone who smoked anything?" I wanted to curse him up one end and down another. In all of these years, I've never chewed a piece of gum in this place. Now I'm going through this. "Sir, I am menstruating right now, and that's the scent the dog is picking up. I have been visiting facilities for probably as long as you have worked here. The dog did not sit down on me, not one time." With a look of disgust in his face he replies, "well, I need you to fill out this form stating you consent to a strip search of your person and vehicle, or you deny the strip search, and you forfeit your visitation for the remainder of the offender's sentence." I held my composure, but this took me to another place.

He handed me the paper, and as I read, he asked, "so are you going to sign it?" I replied, "I consent, but I need your contact information as well as the warden because this is bull shit." He handed me a pen to sign the paper, "give me your information first!" I demanded. He gave the card. I signed it and followed the two female officers in the room. They instructed me to remove one piece of clothing at a time and hand them to the officers, including my underwear and sanitary napkin. I held it together at first, but when it got down to my underwear, I broke. Tears ran down my face. I started to hyperventilate. The room seemed like the walls were closing in on me. I thought the worse was over until I was completely naked and asked to spread my cheeks, squat, and cough. That was it for me. I was so pissed I wanted to fight everyone in there. I maintained my composure because I knew my husband would be the one to suffer the repercussions.

The officers instructed me to get dressed. They both had the look of shame in their faces. I put my clothes on through the tears. I bolted out of the room, trying to find the nearest exit. At that point, I just wanted to leave. But I had completely forgotten about the vehicle search.

Two male guards followed me to my car, where they began to search. As I stood and watched, I cried and cried. I saw one woman who came to visit her husband and told her what happened. Jay Jay had a job in the visitation room, so I knew she would see him when she went in. I told her to let my husband know what was going on and tell him, please don't go crazy. That was all I needed for him to go off and get in trouble. God knows what they may have done to him in there. As the officers completed their search, I said a quick prayer to calm myself down enough to think clearly and take action. Once I said Amen, the officers told me the car was cleared and told me I could go. "You mean you found NOTHING on both searches, and I STILL CAN'T SEE MY HUSBAND?!" They looked at me and walked off; I was PISSED!

I got in the car, slammed the door, and went live on Facebook. I was crying hysterically as I explained to the world everything that happened. The viewers were increasing, and people were sharing the feed repeatedly. I even went back to the office where they strip-searched me and demanded a copy of the paper I signed while I was live on Facebook. I was denied a copy of the document and told I would have to call the number on the card. They pissed me off even more. I completed my live video and cried some more. Our friends and families were watching, and my phone was ringing nonstop. I talked to one of my husband's good friends who had recently come home. He calmed me down enough for me to drive home. I also got a call from a friend of mine who talked to me almost the entire ride home. The day was still early, but so much going on, I was already over it.

The ride from the facility to home was only 40 minutes, but by then, the video had reached over 800 views. I was so tired from crying, but the phone rang and brought back everything I just went through, it was my husband. "Are you alright, baby?!" I had cried so much my voice stifled when I responded. "No!" I said as I started to cry again. The thought of it made me furious. "I know baby," he said. I gave him the play by play of what happened. Eventually, I calmed down enough to muster a smile when he said something funny. My husband had a way of breaking my bad attitude. "Please don't get into trouble, baby. I prayed, and God said its alright." "I'm not, baby. I just want you to be okay. I'm so sorry this happened to you. Let's pray together." And that's what we did. As we said, "Amen," it felt as if a heavenly calm came over me. We reassured each other things were going to be alright and left it at that.

After I talked to my husband, I took a much-needed nap. It took a while for me to settle down. I felt like someone was watching me. When I woke up, I was shocked to find my live video had been seen and shared 3000 times. I had so many comments and inbox messages from people who had encountered the same thing, if not WORSE. The more messages I read, the angrier I became. This time, my anger was for those who suffered similar experiences. I could not believe people had been going through these issues, and their only choice was to "deal with it." I read so many sad stories of elderly mothers going to visit their sons were stripped searched. Some of them who were cancer patients have had mastectomies and other body-altering things which made them ashamed of showing their bodies to strangers. The thought of what they had to bare was nothing less than sickening. Something had to change.

I got a call from a friend whose husband was in the same building as mine. "Jay Jay has been sent to the hole. He went without incident. They came for him while he was asleep, but he did not do anything."

"Thanks for the information, but I already figured something like this might happen." I hung up the phone, cried, and prayed God was in control, but the human in me felt defeated. I allowed myself to process my feelings. Eventually, I laid down and went to bed. I had about all I could take for the day.

That night was rough. I really couldn't sleep well. The residual thoughts of what I went through wouldn't allow me to rest. I honestly wanted to forgive all of whom were involved, but my anger would not let that happen without some work. This time, I was willing to do what it took to shake this feeling and face this challenge head-on. I knew God gave this to me for a purpose. It was up to me to accept the challenge. I ACCEPT.

I woke up the next morning to my notifications going crazy. When I checked my Facebook page, to my surprise, the video had 8000 views. There werepeople in my inbox asking me for interviews and activists ready to take charge. I had one local activist reached out to me. He shared information about my story with the local government officials, the Governor's office, and other families who have experienced injustice. The responses brought tears to my eyes. It was at that moment, my brain clicked into action. My purpose was to provide a voice for those who are in this struggle with me. I was all for it. This fight was for justice, and not just my husband and me. This was about everyone and every family that was doing time.

I wrote emails and made phone calls to officials all day long. Some acknowledgments were immediate. Some never came to this day. At that point, I wasn't concerned about them. I was satisfied with making people aware that we are not taking this abuse anymore. I had a fire lit in my heart to expose the injustices that people were experiencing. My focus was on getting the work done; I couldn't even sleep at night. My husband being in the hole didn't make the situation any better. I knew he was okay, but I missed hearing his voice at night. I knew this was only a test of this journey, a journey that started 21 years ago but was just beginning.

By Wednesday of that week, the facility administration and then the warden contacted me. "My apologies for what happened to you on Sunday. We should never have taken your husband to the hole. You have to understand we have a terrible drug problem at this facility, and I just want it to stop." "I understand sir, but with all due respect, what does your drug problem have to do with my husband and me? He has been infraction free for the last seven years he has been at this facility, and I have been visiting for probably as long as you have been in the service. I have never been through such treatment! Not even at a higher-level security facility!" The conversation went on with the warden explaining he agreed my husband was a very stand up inmate (if that makes sense) and he has never had any trouble out of him. He also told me he offered my husband a transfer to another facility in which my husband declined. I was happy he refused the offer. See, I had done my research on this man. He had several cases at other facilities where there were incidents and inmate complaints against him that resulted in transfers, therefore closing the case. We were not going out like that. Besides, why should he transfer to another facility when this one was the closest step to home. This was an easy way out for the DOC, and they were not going to win again.

hapter thirteen

Thursday morning came, and the phone rang, IT WAS MY HUSBAND. "Hey, babe!!" I felt like a teenager again.

"Hey babe, how are you?"

"Better now!" We talked as if nothing happened at first. We had a silent understanding when it came to any business, we would save to discuss in person. On the phone, it was flowers and butterflies, in person it was about business. Our phone call felt like talking to him for the first time. But this time, we focused on the fact that the worse was over, and we were very grateful for that. We talked, said our normal "I love you's" and then blew air kisses. That conversation was what I needed to start my day.

I went on about my day as usual after I spoke with him. The fire in my heart wouldn't die, though. Something had to be done about this situation. I prayed about it and decided to wait to see my husband face to face before I put a plan in action. I was confident that we would be able to come to a resolution. Besides, he was on the countdown to go home, and I knew that there had to be sure things in place for him to be able to make a smooth transition into this new world. The solution was not only for those who have experienced such injustice. It was therapeutic for those who are coming back into society and need a place to speak about the hurt and pain.

That weekends' visit was the best visit out of many that we have ever had. Not only did I get to see my husband, but I got to see how well he handled the conflict we just survived. His approach to what happened helped me through the anger and pain. I believe he was boiling over on the inside, but throughout the years, he learned to lash out was not the only way to handle a situation. This was a big step for him. I was so proud of his accomplishment. All I could do was stare at him and smile. "Baby, why are you looking at me like that?" he asked with a slight giggle. "I'm so freaking proud of you, Jonathan!!"

We laughed together. "Thank you, babe. I'm proud of you too!"I don't even think we talked about what happened. We enjoyed the remainder of our time and parted ways. Our hearts were content for the day.

The following week, I had invitations to do several interviews with journalists and people who had podcasts to talk about the experience. I received a call to be a guest on a radio show. I took the invite as a break from all the foolery with DOC. The show was great, and at the end of the show, the owner of the station and I had a very detailed conversation about our story. He was very intrigued by it, as most people are. I knew how I was going to have their stories shared, and voices heard. That night when I spoke with my husband, I ran the ideas I came up with him to see what he thought. I knew he was going to stick by me with pretty much anything I said, but I still respected him enough to ask his opinion. He agreed this would be an excellent opportunity to spread the word of what prison life was like and what those who support inmates go through.

I secured the spot and went in headfirst with the show. We decided to call it, From Prison to Promise. I had no idea when we started, that the show would receive the response it did. I met a lot of good people. Through those people, I gained a better understanding of what my husband was going through being incarcerated. I also shared their stories with my husband to remind him that he is not in this alone. Our show created many meaningful relationships with inmates as well as their families. It taught me so much and helped me to see past what inmates have done. Now I'm interested in what they NEED. Not only to make a smooth transition to come home but also to process the hurt and pain they went into prison with, so they can become a better person.

So now that the time is coming for my husband to return to society, we have talked of helping others with the necessary services they require past what prison re-entry programs provide. We hope to have a residential re-entry program that will provide such assistance and give men and women a chance to help themselves as well as others. Our journey has been a rough one, but not without lessons learned. Supporting the incarcerated is not for everyone. Looking back over the years and taking into consideration the lessons we have learned and the changes we have made, I am grateful to be transparent to those who may be walking the same path. Not everyone will agree with the choices you make. Not everyone wants to listen to the stories you have to tell. But when all is said and done, know you are NOT IN THIS ALONE.

Sonya Staples

When the topic of prison reform and reducing recidivism arises in community conversations, one of the top individuals that come to mind is Mrs. Sonya Evan Staples. Mrs. Staples has become a pioneer in bringing awareness to the growing rates of incarcerated citizens and the lack of resources after re-entry into the community.

She is a Richmond native with a passion for community development. Helping the prison community at a grass-root level is her life's work. Mrs. Staples has volunteered for over 20 years and prides herself on being a vehicle of change. She has dedicated her time, energy and resources to building strong individuals and has helped to birth stronger families and communities. Everything she touches is aligned with that mission; from Life Coaching to being a Media Specialist for C.I.R.N, the Criminal Injustice Reform Network.

Sonya Evan Staples is the founder of the non-profit organization "From Prison to Promise. This organization was established in 2017 with the mission of providing a voice to those who have been silenced by incarceration. Weekly, Mrs. Staples gives individuals a safe space to discuss issues surrounding incarceration through the "From Prison to Promise" Internet radio show. It is her hope that individuals impacted by incarceration will gain strength and strategies to alleviate the struggle of waiting or starting over.

When Mrs. Staples is not deep into tackling issues within the prison community she is a wife, mother, notary public and aspiring author.

Each of these tasks further pushes her mission of creating a better community for all.

For business inquires or more, contacted her by email at fromprisontopromise@gmail.com.

Follow the journey:

Facebook : From Prison to Promise

Instagram: @fp_2p

For Bulk Copies, Author Appearances or Publishing Inquiries, please contact ayoka@vogpublishing.com

VOG

PUBLISHING